INTRODUC

Text by
Christina
Coster-Longman

Illustrations by
Ivan Stalio,
Lorenzo Cecchi,
Sauro Giampaia

Human bodies are truly
machines, made up o
that help them funct
responsible for a special type
circulatory system uses the h
full of nutrients and oxygen
The digestive system breaks
the nutrients can be used to
heal, and work properly – an
the waste. We breathe in oxy
carbon dioxide using the res
the skeletal and muscular sys
together and make it move.
working all the time to keep
prepare children's bodies to
become adult bodies. But no
of these systems could possib
work by themselves, or
without the brain and
nervous system to tell them
what to do. The brain is like
a marvellous central
computer, constantly
checking up on the
outside world and
controlling how the
body works. This
book explains some of the
amazing things that are
happening all the time insid
our bodies.

Nerves carry messages to all parts of the body through a special e-mail system, where the messages exchanged are in the form of electric currents. Billions of nerve cells (neurons), in bundles, make up the nerves. Most nerves contain two types of neurons. *Sensory neurons* send signals to the brain about the outside world. They check up on us all the time. They tell us about our position (balance, orientation, etc.), whether our hearts are beating too fast, if we are cold and need to shiver to increase our internal temperature, and so on. *Motor neurons* send signals from the brain to the muscles. But in special cases, our reflexes don't have to travel all the way to the brain.

spinal cord

brain

peripheral nerves

You have 31 pairs of nerves entering the spinal cord and 12 pairs (cranial nerves) in your head.

The nervous system is divided into a *central* and an *autonomic nervous system*. In order for the peripheral nerve to communicate with the central nervous system, they must enter the spinal cord. Precious nerves in the spinal cord are protected by the vertebrae.

THE NERVOUS SYSTEM

The nervous system – the brain, spinal cord, and nerves – is like a computer network receiving and analyzing information from the outside world and from the body, and deciding what actions to take. The brain controls all our mental and physical activities, from things like helping us remember someone's name, reading books, and riding a bicycle, to doing math, and dreaming. We don't have to think about all the things we do though. Our network also controls functions like our body's temperature, digestion, and heartbeat.

MEMORY

Our brains are able to remember, and to forget, an enormous amount of information. There are two main types of memory. Long-term memory is our ability to store information for days, weeks, or even years. But the brain is very selective about what we remember – we sometimes forget important things but retain trivial ones. Short-term memory is used to remember things for short periods of time.

As we read, the information taken in by our eyes is processed in the brain to form an image. This information is then stored in our memories.

SKIN SENSORS: TOUCH

Touch is a very developed sense with blind people, who use the Braille system to read. They do this by feeling, with their fingertips, the shapes and numbers of dots that replace printed words.

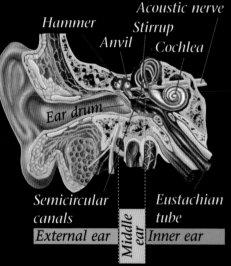

All over your skin are thousands of tiny sensors. These send signals about the temperature, pressure, and texture of anything they come into contact with. This is how you can tell the difference between a cold stone and a cat's warm fur, or feel wind on your face. Hands are very sensitive because they have lots of these sensors very close together.

THE EAR

Acoustic nerve

Hammer   Stirrup

Anvil   Cochlea

Ear drum

Semicircular canals

Eustachian tube

External ear   Middle ear   Inner ear

Our ears have an external, middle, and inner part.

HEARING

A sound travels in all directions from its point of origin, rather like the waves that crimple the surface of a pool when a stone is dropped into the water. Sound waves are captured by the external ear. Then they travel along the ear canal until they reach the eardrum – they make this vibrate. These vibrations pass through three tiny bones in the middle ear and enter a special fluid. When they reach the cochlea, the vibrations cause tiny hairs to trigger signals to the brain. The brain's hearing center interprets the signals so that we know what we are hearing.

SENSE ORGANS

Sense organs tell us about the world around us – they work together to create a complete picture of our surroundings. The main sense organs are: the eyes (which tell us what shapes, colors, and movements we see), the nose (for smelling perfumes and odors), the ears (which hear noises and sounds), the tongue (for tasting), and, the largest of all, the skin (which senses all sorts of touch, like texture, pressure, and temperature). We can also feel pain, which tells us if something is wrong, and we can hear loud noises or see things that might indicate danger. We can taste our food, to make sure that it is good to eat, and smell things around us. So our senses work to keep us out of danger too.

The painting on this page was done by the French artist Claude Monet. He was part of a group of painters called Impressionists who liked to paint nature so vividly that looking at one of their works was almost like being in the picture. Imagine that you could slip into the country scene in this picture. What sense organs do you think you would use?

erves
gnals
e eyes
rain.

TYPES OF MUSCLE

There are three different types of muscle. They are made of different kinds of tissue, and have different purposes.

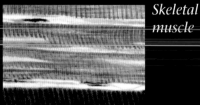

Skeletal muscle

SKELETAL MUSCLES

Skeletal muscles are sometimes called striped muscles because their bundles of fibers have light and dark bands running across them. Skeletal muscles are also called voluntary muscles, because the brain can control them and tell them what to do. Skeletal muscles contract to pull your bones and make you move. Tendons bind them to bones. The big muscles in arms and legs, as well as other parts of the body, are voluntary muscles.

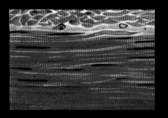

Smooth muscle

SMOOTH MUSCLES

Smooth muscles are found in internal organs like the stomach and intestines, and also in the eyes. These muscles are not attached to bones. Signals from the brain control these muscles automatically, without us having to think about it. That's why they are also called involuntary muscles.

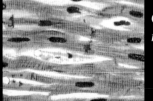

Cardiac muscle

CARDIAC MUSCLES

Cardiac muscle, although also involuntary, is a special sort of muscle that makes the heart pump.

MUSCLES

All of the body's movements are created by muscles. We have about 640 muscles that move our bodies. These muscles are controlled by signals and instructions sent by the brain. Our muscles are working all the time, whether we are playing sport, reading, digesting food, or even just sitting still. As they work, muscles produce heat and so keep our bodies at the right temperature. When we shiver, this is really hundreds of muscles contracting to produce heat.

About two-fifths of the body's weight is made up of muscle. Muscles are controlled by signals from the brain. Big bands of muscle cover the whole body under the skin, and help it to move. Even standing still uses many different muscles, all holding tightly to each other to keep the body upright. The biggest muscle in the body is the gluteus maximus in the buttock – it helps us to run, jump, and climb. The smallest are the muscles in the eyes, and in part of the ear.

WHAT ARE BONES MADE OF?

Many of our bones are soft and elastic when we are born. Cells in the bones gradually deposit a mineral – calcium – that hardens the bones. Bones have different outsides and insides. The cortical bone is on the outside, and is very hard and smooth. Inside this is the hard but spongy cancellous tissue, which makes the bone both light and strong. A soft, jelly-like substance called bone marrow fills the centers of bones. This can be either red or yellow – red marrow can make millions of new blood cells each second.

If our bones break, they can usually mend as long as the broken ends are close together. Calcium salts are deposited to heal the break.

THE SPINE

The spine holds the body upright and also allows us to twist, bend, and move. The spine is made of 33 bones, some fused together. These are shaped like rings, and they are called "vertebrae." There are different kinds of vertebrae in the spine.
– 7 cervical vertebrae support the head and neck.
– 12 thoracic vertebrae hold the ribs in place.
– 5 lumbar vertebrae in the lower back are large and strong, and support a lot of weight.
– The sacrum is a wedge-shaped bone made of 5 fused vertebrae.
– The coccyx, at the bottom of the spine, is made of 4 vertebrae fused together. (In some animals these bones form the tail.)

bends

THE SKELETON

The skeleton holds the body together and protects very important internal organs (such as the brain, heart, lungs, and liver). Without a skeleton, our bodies would have no support and they would flop. The skull and the backbone, also called the axial skeleton, give us our shape. The limbs – part of the appendicular skeleton – are designed for a range of movements. All our bones are linked together through different types of joints that allow us to make all sorts of movements. Our bones are very much alive – they grow and change like other parts of the body.

All the different types of joints in our bodies mean we can twist and turn our bones to make a fantastic variety of movements.

An adult's body has about 206 bones in it. Bones are very important, as they structure the body and allow you to move around in different ways, as well as protecting the body's internal organs.

nt

BLOOD

The human body contains about 12 pints (six liters) of blood. Blood transports important vitamins, chemicals, sugars, hormones, and nutrients throughout the body.

Blood is made up of plasma, red cells, white cells, and platelets. Plasma is mostly water, but also includes proteins, salts, acids, sugars, nutrients, and minerals. White cells fight infection, red blood cells carry oxygen, and platelets help blood to clot. When body tissues are damaged, the platelets release chemicals to make tiny sticky threads out of protein. These threads trap blood cells, building up a clot that prevents more body fluids escaping. It then hardens into a scab to help heal the damage.

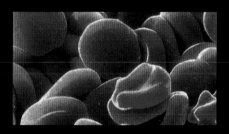

Red blood cells contain iron that can capture oxygen. Their special shape lets them squeeze through tiny capillaries, so they can release oxygen where it is needed.

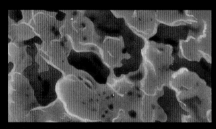

Platelets rush to the rescue, ready to heal cuts and breaks.

White blood cells are able to change shape, so they can move around the body to wherever they are needed to fight germs.

BLOOD AND CIRCULATION

The heart pumps blood around the body's network of blood vessels. This is called circulation. Because blood is fluid and can move easily, it is an excellent carrier of the oxygen and nutrients that we need all around our bodies. Blood also works as a waste collector, by taking carbon dioxide to the lungs. Blood is cleaned in the two kidneys – these wonderful filters, located in the upper rear abdomen, purify our blood by removing any other wastes, so that we can get rid of them in urine.

anx

The circulatory system is like a series of railroad tunnels, with the blood traveling through it like one long, non-stop train. Passengers – like oxygen, minerals, nutrients, and carbon dioxide – are always hopping on and off in different areas of the body. If the circulatory system were laid out straight it would stretch for more than 60,000 miles (100,000 km).

uspid v

Bloo
the b
vess
capi
musc
vess
thin
and
join
carr
retu
arter
and
Bloo
oxyg

Blood is a special, precious tissue. Blood donors can save other people's lives by giving some of their blood. The medical team tapping the donors will check which blood group they belong to: A, B, or O, and whether their blood is Rh positive or negative (Rh+, Rh–).

21

AMAZING AIRWAYS

The respiratory system begins with the nose and mouth, and tubes (windpipe and bronchi) that branch out in the lungs.

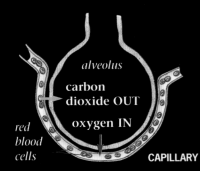

Fresh air enters our airways through our noses or mouths. The airways have many branches (bronchi), which get smaller and thinner, like the branches and twigs of a tree. In the lungs, the bronchioles (smaller tubes) become even finer. The tiniest tubes end in little rounded sacs just one layer thick, called alveoli. These sacs are supplied with capillaries just one-cell-thick. As red blood cells squeeze through capillaries, they pick up oxygen and release carbon dioxide.

Unwrapping lungs into a carpet would almost cover a tennis court!

alveolus

carbon dioxide OUT

oxygen IN

red blood cells

CAPILLARY

There are over 700 million alveoli in our lungs.

The body needs oxygen, but cannot store very much of it. That's why we need to breathe all the time. When we breathe, we absorb oxygen through our lungs, where it is collected by blood and distributed around the body. During this process, blood also picks up the carbon dioxide, a poisonous waste product our cells produce when they use the oxygen. Then our blood releases carbon dioxide into the lungs and we expel it when we breathe out.

BREATHING

Our bodies always need fresh supplies of oxygen – this is why we have to breathe all the time. Our breathing varies according to our needs: an average adult breathes in and out about 16 times every minute, children usually breathe faster. When we are asleep, our breathing is shallow because we need less oxygen. But during or after intense exercise, like running, we breathe faster and deeper – between 30 and 60 breaths each minute. Some people – like singers, wind instrument players, and snorklers – train so that they can hold more air in their lungs.

High in the mountains, the air contains less oxygen. If you travel up into the mountains, your body begins to make more red blood cells so that your blood can capture more oxygen from the air you breathe.

ndpipe

ioles

Left

THE DIGESTION JOURNEY

Food has to go on a very long journey to be absorbed by the body. We start digesting food the minute we put it into our mouths. Teeth cut and chew solid food (like bread, meat, and fruit) into smaller pieces so it can be broken down better by the special digestive juices it will meet on its journey. The first juice food meets is saliva, which helps digest starchy food like bread and cookies (carbohydrates.) Saliva also makes food moist and soft, so it is easy to swallow.

The tongue pushes chewed food back into the pharynx (throat). The whole of the digestive tract is lined with powerful muscles that push food along on its way, so we can digest our food no matter what position we are in, even upside down!

Food is forced down the oesophagus to the stomach. The stomach's contracting walls pulp the food into an almost liquid mass. This is where we start digesting proteins (such as milk, cheese, and meat).

As food enters the intestine, enzymes (special juices that help digest different sorts of nutrients) break it down even further. The small intestine begins to absorb the food. Here, a frilly wall-lining – with as many as 500 microscopic "fingers" (villi and microvilli) per square inch – absorbs the nutrients into the blood stream. In the large intestine, where enzymes are no longer produced and digestion is almost over, we mainly absorb minerals and water. We are left with a heavy liquid mass, like thick soup. This is sent to the rectum, where the solid waste materials, called feces, are collected. The feces are then expelled through the anus.

THE DIGESTIVE SYSTEM

The food you eat provides your body with the fuel it needs to work properly and the building blocks it uses to grow. But without the digestive system, the body would not be able to extract important nutrients and fuels from the food. The digestive tract is a long tunnel with many different areas and sections, almost like a very long and twisty waterslide. As food is pushed along through this system, special organs (like the stomach, pancreas, and liver) help the body to extract all the goodness (such as carbohydrates, fats, and proteins) that it needs.

As you pass by a bakery, with the smell of fresh bread wafting out the door, or stop at a colorful market stall displaying all sorts of delicious fruit, or even think of something tasty to eat or drink, your mouth may start watering. The water in your mouth is saliva, the first secretion for helping your body to digest food.

...ach squashes foo...
...t together with ...
...enzymes.

...eas makes
...juices, to
...igestion,
...them into
...ntestine
...num.)

...es open the anus t...
...waste matter, in th...
...f feces.

The stomach is like a sac, with strong muscular walls. These walls contract, churning the food and mixing it with gastric juices (made of acids, water, enzymes, and mucus) to break it down even further. The partly digested food then travels on to the intestines.

29

This child has dark hair and dark eyes like its parents.

What a person looks like depends a lot on their genes. Human life starts as one fertilized egg, but inside that egg are all the instructions (genes) for the body's development and growth. Altogether we have from 50,000 to 100,000 genes that we inherit; half come from the mother and half from the father. Genes decide things like the color of hair, eyes, and skin, how tall we will be and whether we will be boys or girls.

This newborn baby is a boy. Gender is determined by genes.

Although every person has a mixture of genes from both their parents, some genes are stronger than others. Even if your mother's or father's eyes are blue, yours may be dark – the genes for blue eyes are not as strong as the genes for darker eyes.

Your hair may be naturally curly or straight, your skin may be pale or dark, your eyes may be blue, brown, or green; all these things and more depend on your genes.

A NEW LIFE

B oys' and girls' bodies are made differently so, as adults, they can reproduce and bring new life into the world. New babies grow inside their mothers. When they are born they feed on their mother's milk. New babies are complete little humans, who need all their parents' love and care. As babies grow, they may be very like their parents in some ways, but as independent individuals they will also reflect the surroundings they have lived in.

nine months
orn. Inside th
its head is p
born headfirs

Humans
women h
breasts,
provides
all of the
needs to
system b
diseases
glands, a
nipples.
where to

SKIN AND HAIR

Skin is the body's barrier against the outside world. Skin has three layers: the *epidermis*, the *dermis*, and the *subcutaneous*. On the outside (epidermis) 30–40,000 dead cells flake off every minute – but don't worry about your skin disappearing, many new skin cells are being formed all the time. The dermis contains special glands that produce oil to protect our skin and keep it water resistant. They also regulate the body's temperature, using sweat – when it is hot, sweat evaporates on the surface of the skin to cool it down. The subcutaneous, the layer where hair follicles are located, is mostly fat to keep us warm.

OUR SKIN (CROSS-SECTION)

Sweat Hair Hair Sebaceous
pore   shaft gland

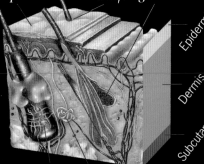

Epidermis

Dermis

Subcutaneous

Hair follicle
Sweat gland   Arrector pili
              muscle

The body (not just the top of the head) is almost entirely covered in hair. Hairs grow inside follicles in the deepest layer of the skin. They grow longer as new cells are added to the root at the bottom of the hair shaft. Once it is outside the skin, hair is really just long strings of dead cells. Oil from the sebaceous glands keeps it glossy.
We have over 100,000 hairs on our heads, and we lose about 50-100 hairs every day. Hair grows about half an inch a month. Tiny body hairs help us keep warm. When we are cold we get goose-pimples, because hair muscles contract and force the hairs to stand up on end to trap warm air close to the skin.

UNDER THE MICROSCOPE

Our bodies are made up of millions and millions of cells with many different shapes, sizes, and tasks. Single cells are so tiny we can't see them with the naked eye. Your school microscope will help you to see different sorts of cells, like those that make up skin or hair. To explore the inside parts of a cell, scientists use very powerful microscopes in the laboratory.

VERY SPECIAL CELLS: THE IMMUNE SYSTEM

The body's lymphatic system helps fight infection to keep us healthy, and it filters out germs and poisons. The lymphatic system carries special "soldier" cells to parts of the body where they are needed. Eighty percent of these soldier cells are called T-cells. Some can live for a long time, and recognize germs they have fought in the past so they can quickly destroy them again.
Macrophages (meaning "big-eaters") engulf any foreign substances that they find.

clean up the
ecycling all t

Would you ever think that these strange "monsters" are running around in our blood? Really, these special T-cells are very friendly, and patrol the body to check up on invaders like germs and viruses.

INDEX